MW01071005

Read & Understand
Understand
WITH LEVELED TEXTS

Grade **K**

Writing: Jill Norris
Content Editing: Joy Evans
De Gibbs
Copy Editing: Carrie Gwynne
Art Direction: Cheryl Puckett
Cover Design: Liliana Potigian
Illustration: Jo Larsen
Design/Production: Yuki Meyer

Evan-Moor
EDUCATIONAL PUBLISHERS
Helping Children Learn since 1979

EMC 3440

Congratulations on your purchase of some of the finest teaching materials in the world.

For information about other Evan-Moor products, call 1-800-777-4362, fax 1-800-777-4332, or visit our Web site, www.evan-moor.com. Entire contents © 2010 EVAN-MOOR CORP. 18 Lower Ragsdale Drive, Monterey, CA 93940-5746. Printed in USA.

Correlated
to State Standards

Visit *teaching-standards.com* to view a correlation of this book's activities to your state's standards. This is a free service.

CPSIA: Printed by McNaughton & Gunn, Saline, MI USA. [10/2009]

Contents

Read and Understand with Leveled Texts, Grade K • EMC 3440 • © Evan-Moor Corp.

How to Use This Book

1 Make the Story Booklets

Reproduce each story and make booklets for individual students. Use the booklets to

- read to a group.
- have partners or small groups read together.
- have individual students read independently.

The stories support Guided Reading levels A, B, and C, with text ranging from simple words that name pictures (for pre-readers) to short sentences (for emergent readers).

2 Build Background

Relating a story to prior knowledge and experiences helps students better comprehend the story. Ask questions that invite students to tell what they know. For example:

- Before reading *Time to Go*, ask students how they get ready to go somewhere.
- Before reading *The Pet Store*, ask: *Have you ever visited a pet store? What animals did you see? Where were the animals kept?*

Concrete experiences also help students develop knowledge of a subject and its related vocabulary. For example:

- Before reading *My Beads*, show students how to make patterns with colored beads.
- Before reading *My Kite*, fly a kite on the playground.

3 Preview the Story

- Read the title of the story and have the students repeat it. Run your finger under the words as you read them to emphasize left-to-right movement.
- Introduce the words in the story's Picture Dictionary and encourage students to watch for the words in the story. Write the words on the board as you talk about them or ask students to locate a word on a specific page.
- Go through the story page by page. Have students look at the illustrations and ask them to predict what they think is happening on each page.

4 Read the Story

When reading the story to students for the first time, read with expression and pronounce words clearly. Invite students to read repeated or familiar words, phrases, or sentences with you. Then encourage students to read lines independently.

5 Do the Skill Pages

Use the skill pages after reading each story to

- assess comprehension.
- reinforce emergent reading skills.
- develop and practice oral and written language.

Before expecting students to work independently, read the directions for each activity and model appropriate responses. The Skills Chart on page 4 provides an overview of the skills practiced in the activities. The focus skills for each activity are printed at the bottom of the worksheet.

Skills Chart

Stories	Letter/sound association	Visual discrimination	Following patterns	Classifying	Rhyming words	Word families	Singular and plural	Following directions	Retelling a story	Answering questions	Recalling story details	Critical thinking	Sequencing	Real and make-believe	Word meaning	Color and number words	Positional words	Small motor skills	Prewriting	Opposites	Matching text to pictures
One or Two?	•										•	•				•					
Up and Down		•						•			•				•	•	•		•		•
Time to Go	•							•			•							•			•
The Pet Store	•							•		•	•	•				•					
My Cat	•	•						•		•	•										
Where Do I Sleep?	•							•			•				•				•		
Go for a Ride	•							•		•	•	•				•					
Cars	•							•			•				•	•		•	•		•
Can You?					•			•			•				•			•	•		
So Many Hats	•				•						•	•							•		
Animal Babies								•			•		•	•					•		
Growing Up					•						•			•					•		
Trucks	•	•								•	•	•			•			•	•		•
Bath Time							•	•			•	•			•				•		
The Colors	•	•						•								•					
My Beads			•		•			•			•					•					
The Ballgame	•			•					•		•	•							•		
My Fish					•				•		•					•				•	
In the Car					•	•					•	•			•					•	
Get in Line		•				•					•		•		•						
Count the Pups	•						•			•	•					•					•
What Do You See?					•	•					•						•	•			
Little Quackers	•							•			•	•									
My Kite	•							•	•		•	•						•	•		
We Have Fun	•								•				•		•				•	•	

4 Read and Understand with Leveled Texts, Grade K • EMC 3440 • © Evan-Moor Corp.

Name _____

On the Slide

Draw yourself on the slide.

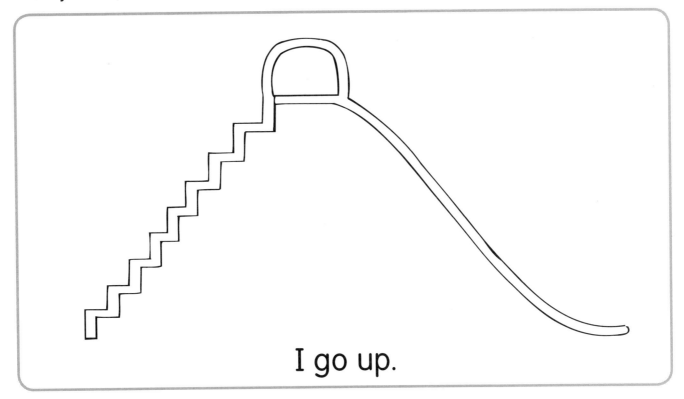

I go up.

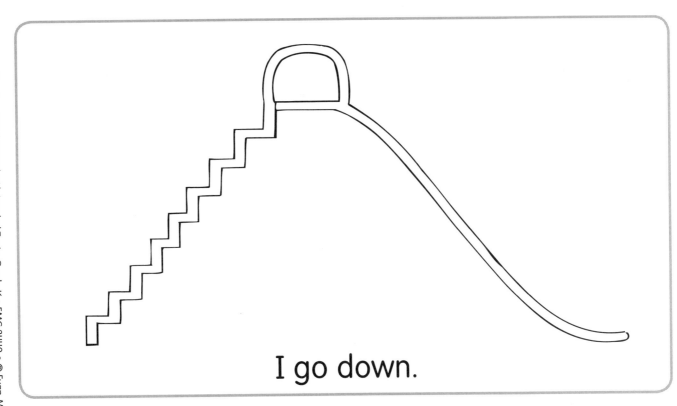

I go down.

 coat

 hat

 dad

Time to Go

_____
Name

1

I get my coat.

I get my hat.

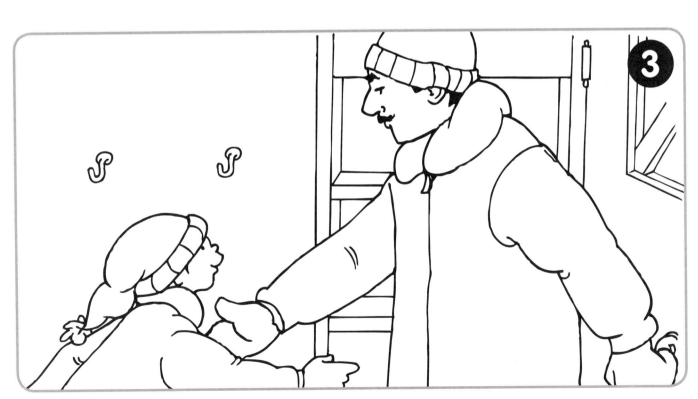

I get my dad.
Time to go.

Remembering the Story

Draw lines to tell what happened in the story.

- I get my boat.

- I get my coat.

- I get my hat.

- I get my cat.

- I get my mom.

- I get my dad.

Skills: Recall story details; match text to pictures.

Read and Understand with Leveled Texts, Grade K • EMC 3440 • © Evan-Moor Corp.

Hang Them Up

Cut and glue.

glue
See my coat.

glue
See my hat.

Skills: Follow directions; match text to pictures.   21

Down the Hill

Draw a line to help them go down the hill.

Skill: Practice small motor skills.

Read and Understand with Leveled Texts, Grade K • EMC 3440 • © Evan-Moor Corp.

Same Sound ···················· **Dd**

Color the pictures that begin like **dad**.

How many did you find?

 dog

 cat

 lizard

The Pet Store

_____
Name

Pet Store

1

I see a dog.
Hi, dog.

I see a cat.
Hi, cat.

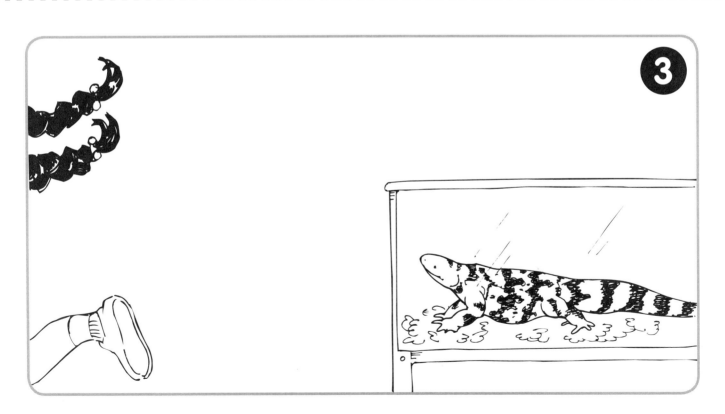

I see a lizard.
Goodbye, lizard!

Remembering the Story

Circle the pictures that answer the questions.

Which animals did the girl see?

Which animals did the girl like?

Which animal made the girl run away?

Which animal would you like for a pet?

Read and Understand with Leveled Texts, Grade K • EMC 3440 • © Evan-Moor Corp.

Name _____

Where Do the Animals Go?

Cut and glue. Lift the cover to look inside.

Skill: Practice critical thinking. **27**

Same Sound · · · · · · · · · · · · · · · · · Cc

Cut and glue the pictures that begin like **cat**.

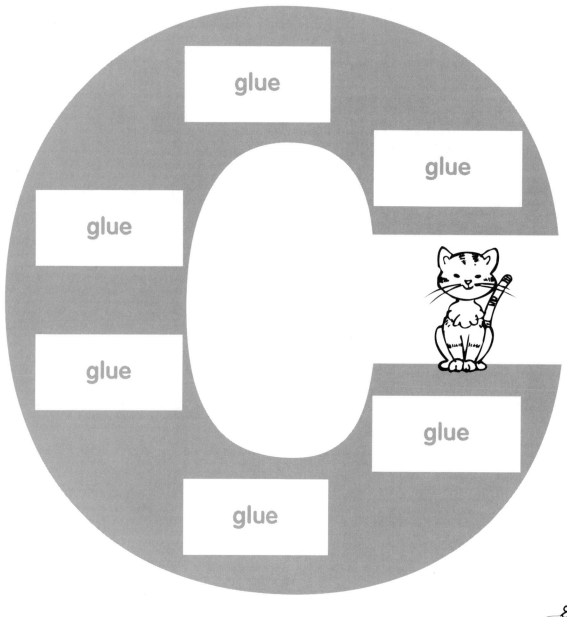

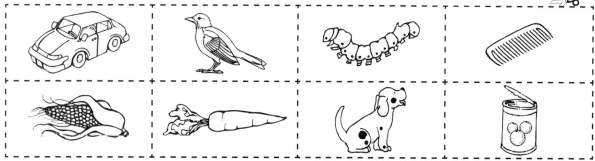

Skill: Letter/sound association.

Read and Understand with Leveled Texts, Grade K • EMC 3440 • © Evan-Moor Corp.

Color Fun

Read the words. Color the picture.

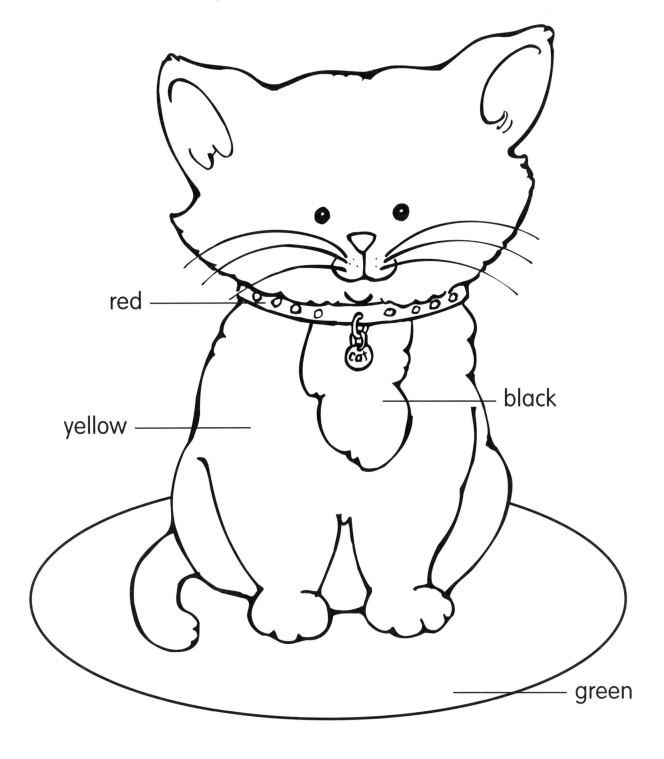

red

black

yellow

green

I see a cat.

Skills: Follow directions; read color words.   **29**

jump

play

sleep

My Cat

_____
Name

My cat likes to jump.

My cat likes to play.

Purr...

My cat likes to sleep.

Name _____

Remembering the Story

Finish each sentence. Color the picture that matches the story.

The cat likes to _____.

The cat has a _____.

At the end, the cat _____.

Read and Understand with Leveled Texts, Grade K • EMC 3440 • © Evan-Moor Corp.

Same Sound ···················· **Jj**

Cut and glue the pictures that begin like **jump**.

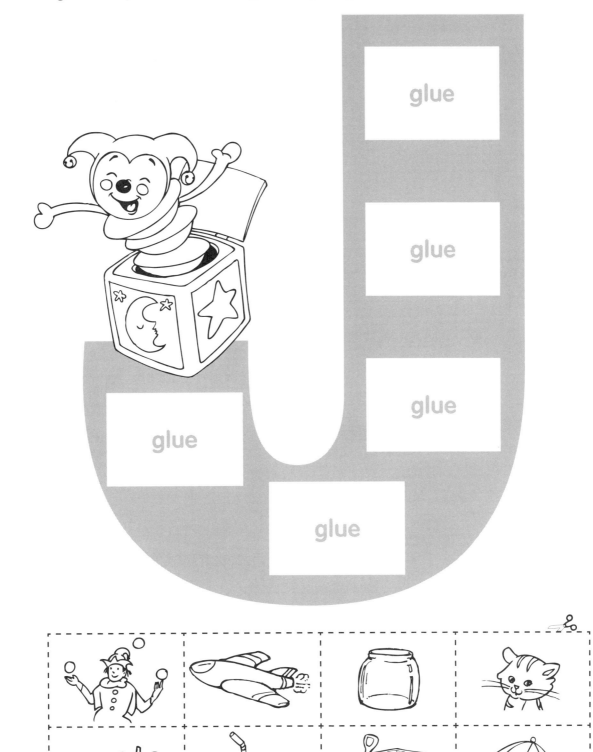

glue

glue

glue

glue

glue

Skill: Letter/sound association. **33**

Same Words

Circle the words in each row that are the same as the first word in the row.

jump	jump	run	jump
play	purr	play	play
sleep	sleep	slow	sleep
meow	man	mom	meow
cat	cat	cat	car

Read and Understand with Leveled Texts, Grade K • EMC 3440 • © Evan-Moor Corp.

My Pet

Draw a picture of a pet.

Color a happy face or a sad face to answer each question.

Does your pet like to jump?

Does your pet like to play?

Does your pet meow?

Skills: Follow directions; answer questions.

 nest

 den

 bed

Where Do I Sleep?

_____
Name

1

I sleep in a nest.

I sleep in a den.

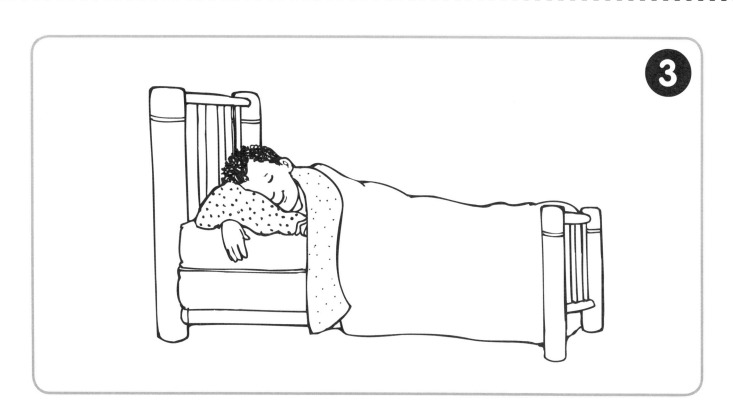

I sleep in a bed.

Remembering the Story

Draw lines to show where they sleep.

den

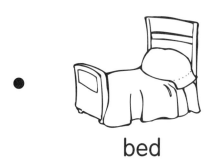

bed

nest

Draw where you sleep.

Read and Understand with Leveled Texts, Grade K • EMC 3440 • © Evan-Moor Corp.

Same Sound ···················· **Bb**

Color the pictures that begin like **boy**.

How many did you find?

Skill: Letter/sound association. **39**

Name _____

Are You Sleeping?

Cut and glue the pictures to show **asleep** and **awake**.

asleep

glue	glue
glue	glue

awake

glue	glue
glue	glue

Skill: Practice word meaning.

Read and Understand with Leveled Texts, Grade K • EMC 3440 • © Evan-Moor Corp.

Name _____

Listen and Draw

Draw a blue balloon in box 1. Draw a yellow triangle in box 2.
Draw a happy face in box 3. Draw a red bed in box 4.

4

Do you sleep in a red bed?   yes   no

Skills: Follow directions; prewriting activity.   41

Picture Dictionary

 **wagon**

 **car**

 **plane**

Go for a Ride

_____

Name

1

We ride in a wagon.

We ride in a car.

We ride in a plane.

Remembering the Story

Circle what they rode in.

wagon

bike

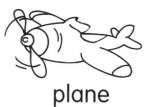

plane

car

truck

Circle the pictures to answer the questions.

Who rode in the wagon?

Who rode in the plane?

Who rode in the car?

44   **Skills:** Answer questions to recall story details.

Read and Understand with Leveled Texts, Grade K • EMC 3440 • © Evan-Moor Corp.

Name _____

Same Sound ···················· Ww

Cut and glue the pictures that begin like **wagon**.

Skill: Letter/sound association.   **45**

Color Fun

Follow the directions to color.

Color the car **red**.

Color the wagon **blue**.

Color the plane **green**.

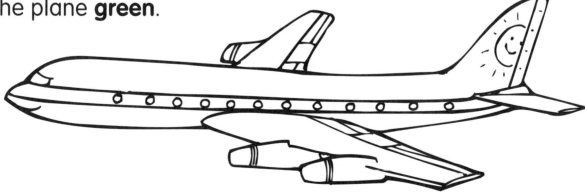

Skills: Follow directions; read color words.

Read and Understand with Leveled Texts, Grade K • EMC 3440 • © Evan-Moor Corp.

Name _____

I Can Ride

Circle what could take you for a ride.

lion

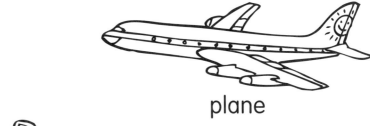

plane

wagon

bike

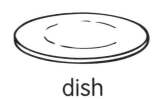

dish

horse

hat

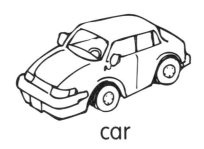

car

skateboard

Skill: Practice critical thinking. **47**

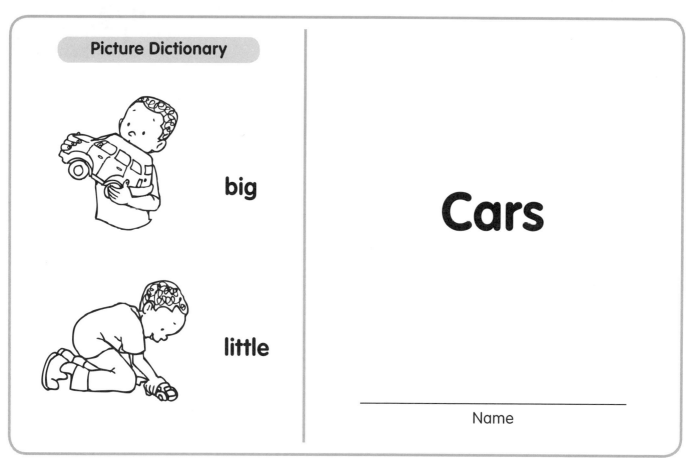

big

little

Cars

_____
Name

1

Look at the big car.

Look at the little cars.

Look at the big and little cars.

Remembering the Story

Draw lines to show which picture matches each sentence.

I see one big car.

•

I see one little car.

•

I see big and little cars.

•

Draw your favorite car. Is it big or little?

Skills: Recall story details; prewriting activity.

Read and Understand with Leveled Texts, Grade K • EMC 3440 • © Evan-Moor Corp.

Name _____

How Many?

Cut and glue to match the pictures and the words.

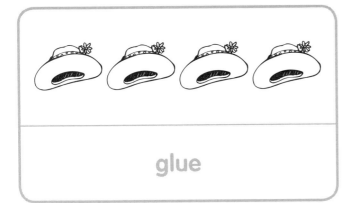

glue

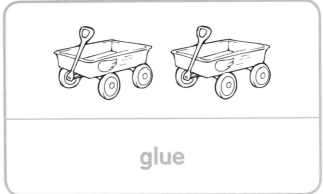

glue

glue

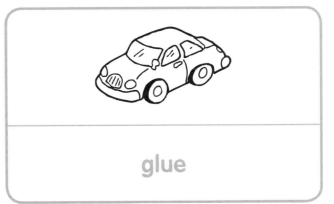

glue

glue

glue

3 cars	1 hat	1 wagon
4 hats	2 wagons	1 car

Skill: Match text to pictures.   51

Big and Little

Trace **big** and **little**.

 big

 little

Write **big** or **little** on the lines.
Tell about the big and little things in the pictures. Color the pictures.

I see one _____ elephant.
It is gray.

I see four _____ bugs.
They are red.

Skills: Practice small motor skills; follow directions; practice word meaning; prewriting activity; read color words.

Read and Understand with Leveled Texts, Grade K • EMC 3440 • © Evan-Moor Corp.

Same Sound ⋯⋯⋯⋯⋯⋯ Ll

Cut and glue the pictures that begin like **lion**.

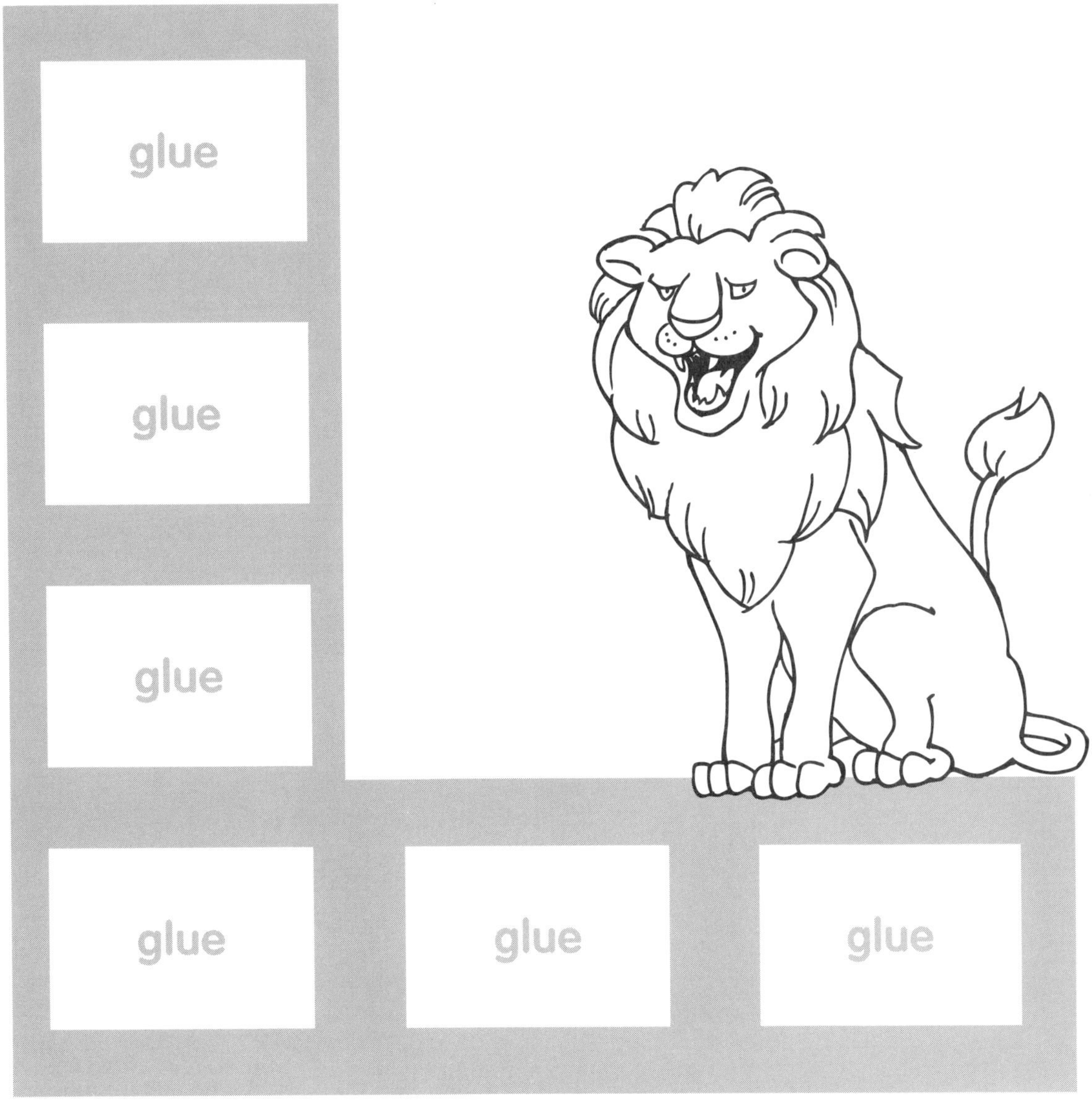

glue

glue

glue

glue glue glue

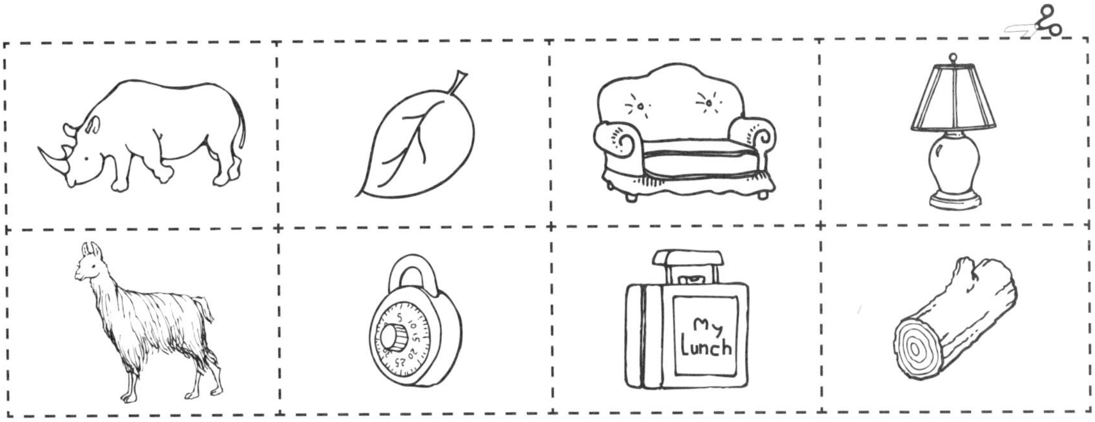

Skill: Letter/sound association. **53**

Picture Dictionary

 run

 hop

 jump

 stop

Can You?

_____
Name

I can run.   I can hop.

1

I can jump.

I can stop.

Circle **yes** or **no**.

Can you run?	yes	no
Can you hop?	yes	no
Can you jump?	yes	no
Can you stop?	yes	no

Good for you!

Remembering the Story

Cut and glue to show what happened in the story.

| glue | **run** |
| glue | **hop** |

| glue | **jump** |
| glue | **stop** |

Skills: Recall story details; practice word meaning.

Read and Understand with Leveled Texts, Grade K • EMC 3440 • © Evan-Moor Corp.

All About You

Draw and write what you can do.

I can _____

_____

_____.

Words That Rhyme

Circle the words that rhyme in each row.

hop

down

shop

stop

mop

jump

top

pop

run

Read and Understand with Leveled Texts, Grade K • EMC 3440 • © Evan-Moor Corp.

What Is It?

Connect the dots. Start at **1**.
What is it? Color it red.

1 •————————• 15

2 •

14 •

3 •

• 13

STOP

4 •

• 12

5 •

• 11

6 •

10 •

7 •

8 •

9 •

Read and Understand with Leveled Texts, Grade K • EMC 3440 • © Evan-Moor Corp.

work hat

 **play** hat

 **sun** hat

 **fun** hat

So Many Hats

_____
Name

I have a work hat.   I have a play hat.

I have a sun hat.   I have a fun hat.

I have so many hats.

Remembering the Story

Circle the hats in the story.

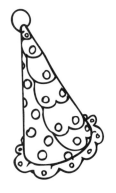

Draw the hat you like the best.

Skills: Recall story details; prewriting activity.

Read and Understand with Leveled Texts, Grade K • EMC 3440 • © Evan-Moor Corp.

Name _____

They Rhyme with Hat

Cut and glue to show the pictures that rhyme with **hat**.

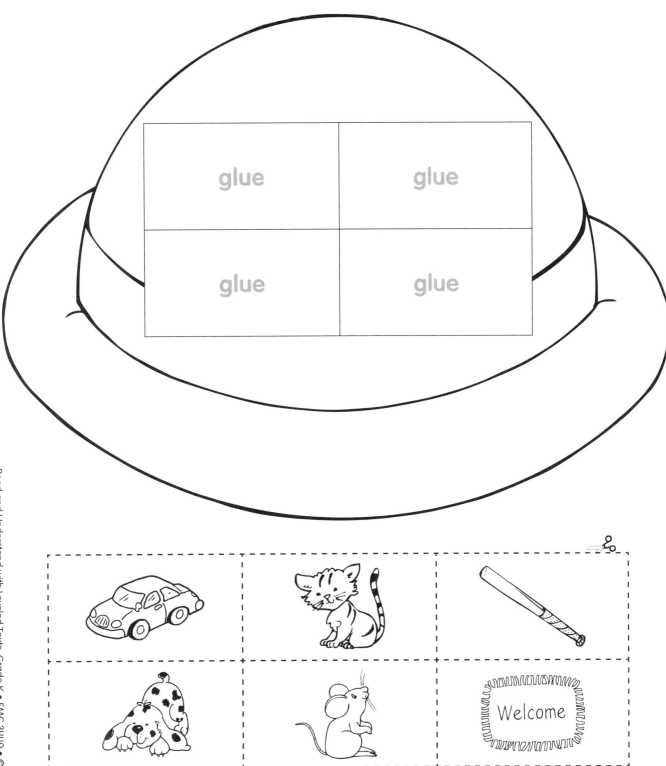

glue glue

glue glue

Read and Understand with Leveled Texts, Grade K • EMC 3440 • © Evan-Moor Corp.

Name _____

Whose Hat?

Draw lines to show who the hats belong to.

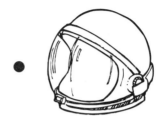

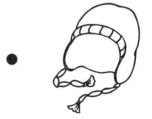

Name _____

Same Sound ···················· Hh

Color the pictures that begin like **hat**.

How many did you find?

cow

 dog

 cat

 bear

Animal Babies

_____
Name

I am a cow.
I have a calf.

I am a dog.
I have a pup.

I am a cat.
I have a kitten.

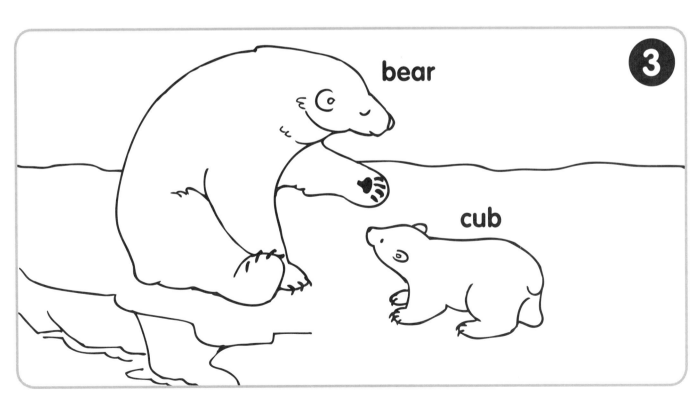

I am a bear.
I have a cub.

Remembering the Story

Draw lines to match the animal parents with their babies.

cub

kitten

pup

calf

Read and Understand with Leveled Texts, Grade K • EMC 3440 • © Evan-Moor Corp.

Name _____

Is It Real?

Look at each picture. Could it happen?
Circle **yes** or **no**.

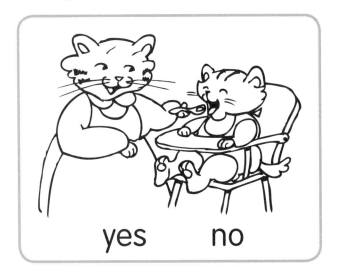

yes   no

yes   no

yes   no

yes   no

yes   no

yes   no

Skill: Distinguish between real and make-believe.   **69**

Growing Up

Cut and glue the pictures in order to show the puppy growing up.

1

glue

2

glue

3

glue

4

glue

Read and Understand with Leveled Texts, Grade K • EMC 3440 • © Evan-Moor Corp.

Make a Mini-Book

Finish the pictures. Cut and staple to make your own little book.

My Animal Book

Name

bear

cat

cow

dog

Match

cow   •

bear   •

dog   •

cat   •

Skills: Follow directions; prewriting activity.   **71**

 shoe

 glue

Growing Up

_____
Name

1

I am growing up.
I can tie my shoe.

I am growing up.
I can use the glue.

I am growing up.
I can read to you.

Remembering the Story

Draw the three things in the story that the children can do.

Skill: Recall story details.

Make a New Page

Draw, write, and cut to make a new page for *Growing Up*.

- -

4

I am growing up.

I can _____.

- -

Growing Up

Cut and glue the pictures in order to show the girl growing up.

1

glue

2

glue

3

glue

4

glue

Read and Understand with Leveled Texts, Grade K • EMC 3440 • © Evan-Moor Corp.

Words That Rhyme

Circle the pictures that rhyme in each row.

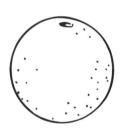  

 **pickup truck**

 **dump truck**

 **firetruck**

Trucks

_____
Name

1

This is a pickup truck.
It can help us.

This is a dump truck.
It can help us.

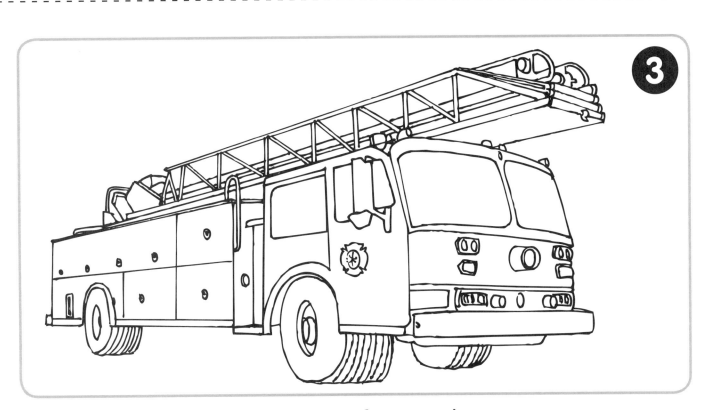

This is a firetruck.
It can help us.

Remembering the Story

Circle to answer the questions.

Which picture shows what the story is about?

What can trucks do?

jump   help us   play

Draw to answer the question.

Where will the firetruck go?

Skills: Recall story details; answer questions; practice critical thinking; prewriting activity.

Read and Understand with Leveled Texts, Grade K • EMC 3440 • © Evan-Moor Corp.

Same Sound ····················· **tr**

Color the pictures that begin like **truck**.

How many did you find?

Name _____

Put the Trucks Together

Cut out the pictures and match the truck parts.
Glue the matching parts side by side on a piece of paper.

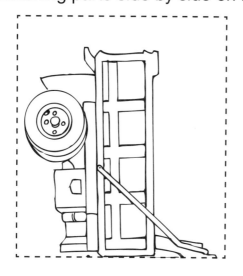

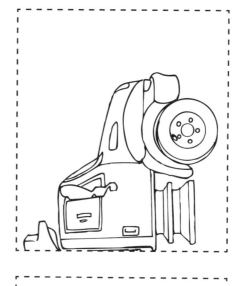

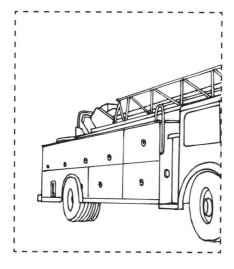

Skills: Visual discrimination; practice small motor skills.

Read and Understand with Leveled Texts, Grade K • EMC 3440 • © Evan-Moor Corp.

They Can Help Us

Circle the word **truck**. How many did you find?

```
b  k  t  r  u  c  k  p
a  p  e  b  x  t  r  a
t  r  d  u  m  r  u  n
r  o  w  t  r  u  c  k
u  b  a  t  s  c  h  c
c  t  r  u  c  k  t  o
k  i  t  n  o  w  z  i
r  m  s  h  v  f  u  n
```

Write the name of each truck on the line.

| dump | fire | pickup |

_____truck   _____ truck   _____ truck

Skills: Visual discrimination; practice word meaning; match text to pictures.   **83**

 **bird**

 **bath**

 **splash**

Bath Time

_____

Name

The bird takes a bath. Splash!

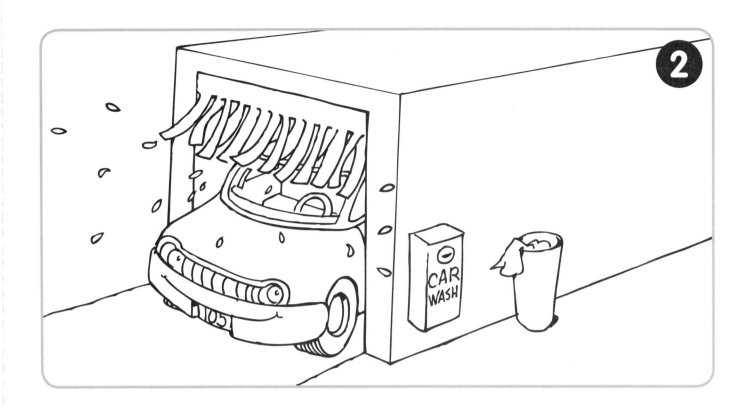

The car gets a bath. Splash!

I take a bath. Splash!
Mom gets a bath, too.

Remembering the Story

Circle **yes** or **no** to tell what happened in the story.

A bird takes a bath.	yes	no
A car gets a bath.	yes	no
A cat takes a bath.	yes	no

Draw to show what happened to Mom.

Read and Understand with Leveled Texts, Grade K • EMC 3440 • © Evan-Moor Corp.

The -ar Family

Write the words. Draw to show what each word means.

c + ar = _____ _____ _____

Draw a car.

j + ar = _____ _____ _____

Draw a jar.

st + ar = _____ _____ _____ _____

Draw a star.

b + ar = _____ _____ _____

Draw monkey bars.

Skills: Word family activity; practice word meaning; follow directions.

Where Do They Take a Bath?

Cut and glue to show where each one might take a bath.

glue

glue

glue

glue

glue

glue

Read and Understand with Leveled Texts, Grade K • EMC 3440 • © Evan-Moor Corp.

A Funny Bath

Draw a funny bath.

Write or tell about the funny bath.

_____

_____

_____

_____

_____

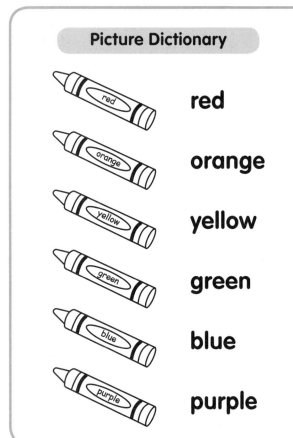

red

orange

yellow

green

blue

purple

The Colors

_____
Name

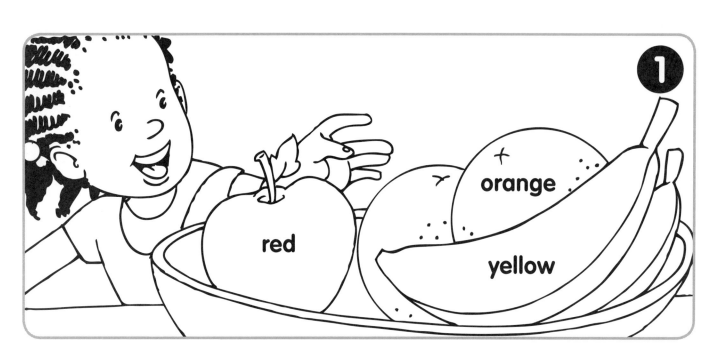

red

orange

yellow

Do you see something red?
Do you see something orange?
Do you see something yellow?

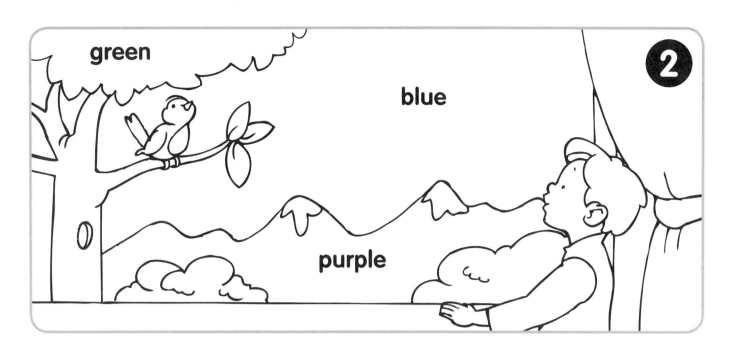

green

blue

purple

Do you see something green?
Do you see something blue?
Do you see something purple?

Do you see all the colors?

Color Fun

Read the words. Color the fruit.

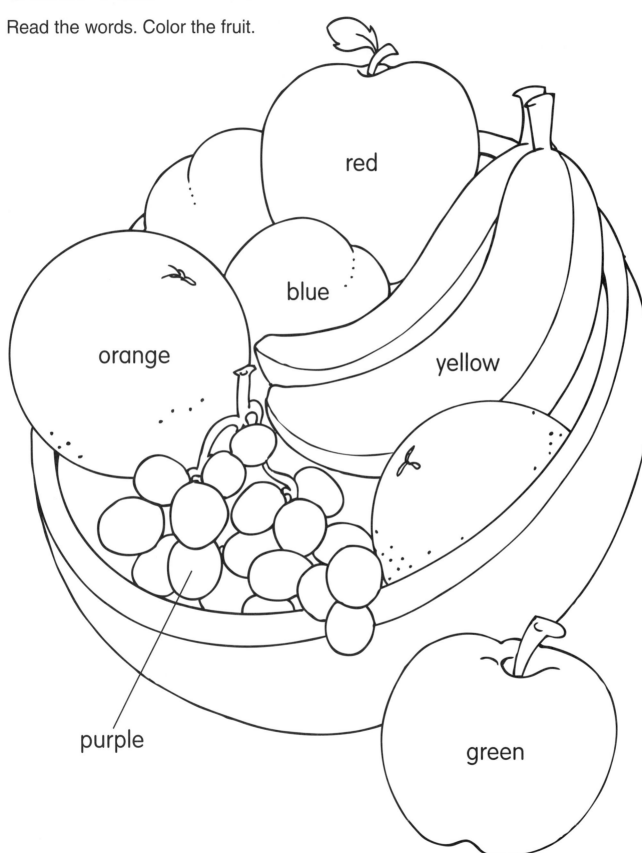

red

blue

orange

yellow

purple

green

Skill: Read color words.

Read and Understand with Leveled Texts, Grade K • EMC 3440 • © Evan-Moor Corp.

Name _____

Same Sound ···················· Yy

Cut and glue the pictures that begin like **yellow**.

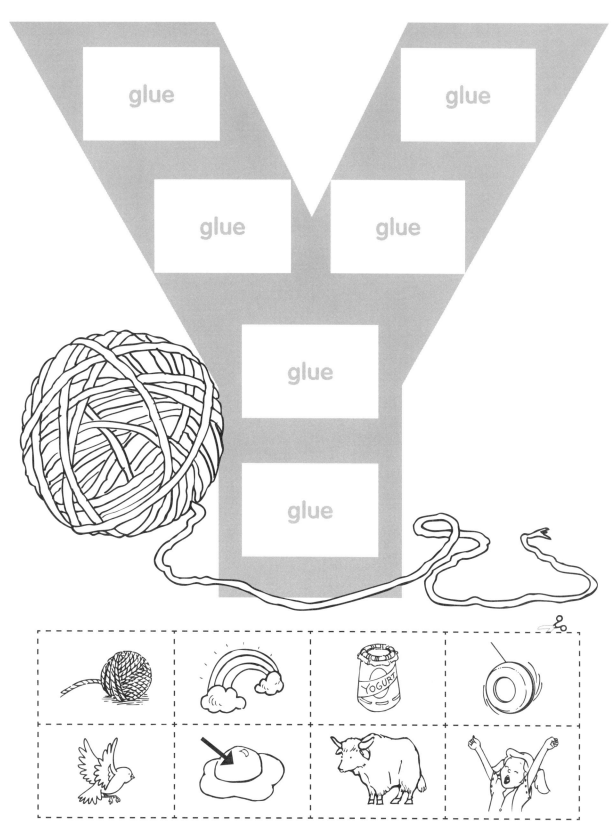

Skill: Letter/sound association.   **93**

Seeing Words

Circle the words in each row that are the same as the first word in the row.

red	run	red	red
yellow	yellow	yarn	yellow
blue	ball	blue	blue
orange	orange	orange	jump
green	get	green	green
purple	purple	play	purple

Skills: Read color words; visual discrimination; follow directions.

Name _____

How Many Do You See?

Write to tell how many you see. Then color the pictures.

one	two	three
four	five	six

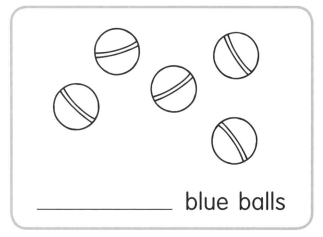

_____ blue balls

_____ yellow ducks

_____ orange socks

_____ purple car

_____ green hats

_____ red bugs

Skills: Read color and number words; follow directions.

red bead

 blue bead

My Beads

_____
Name

1

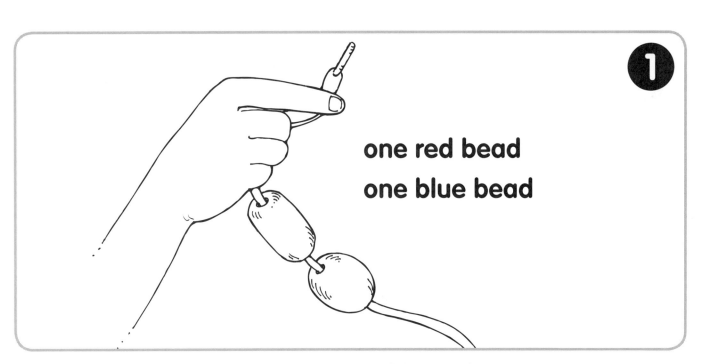

one red bead
one blue bead

I have one red bead.
I have one blue bead.
I have two beads.

one red bead

one blue bead

one red bead

one blue bead

I have one more red bead.
I have one more blue bead.
Now I have four beads.

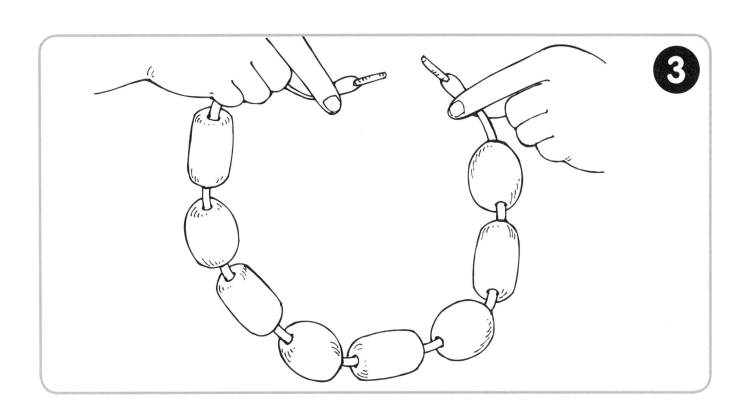

Look at all my red and blue beads.

Remembering the Story

Color, cut, and glue to match the story.

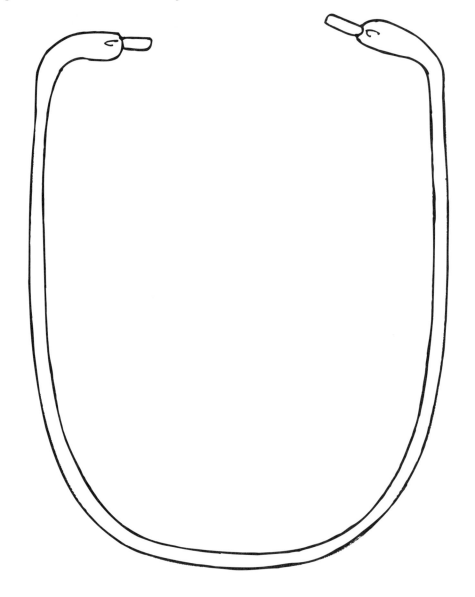

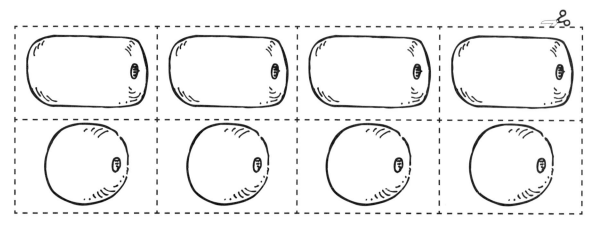

Skills: Recall story details; make a pattern.

Read and Understand with Leveled Texts, Grade K • EMC 3440 • © Evan-Moor Corp.

How Many Beads?

Write to tell how many beads you see.
Then color the beads.

one	two	three
four	five	six

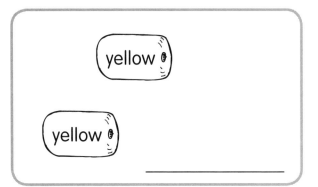

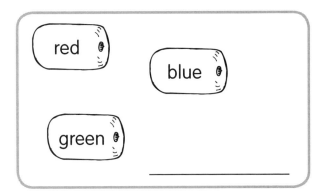

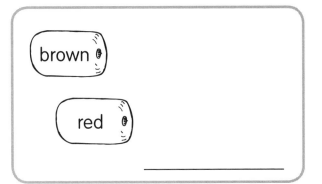

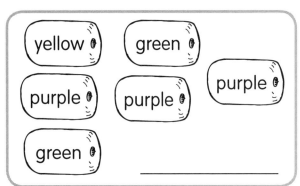

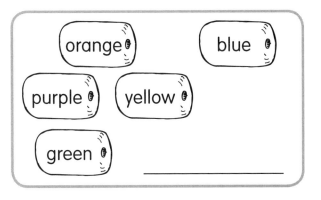

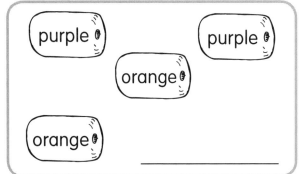

Skills: Read number and color words; follow directions.   **99**

Make a Pattern

Color the beads to finish the pattern.

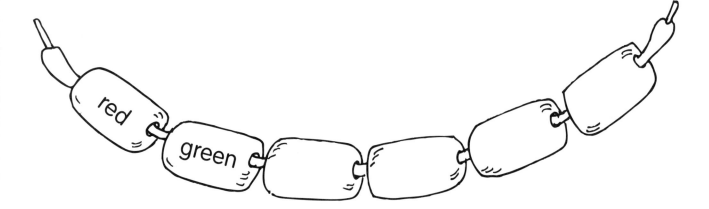

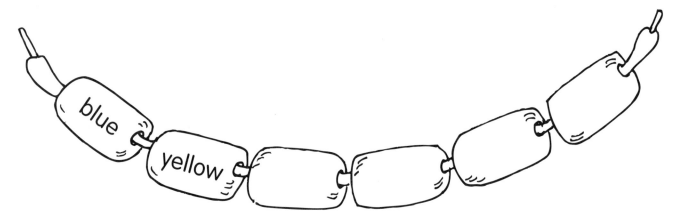

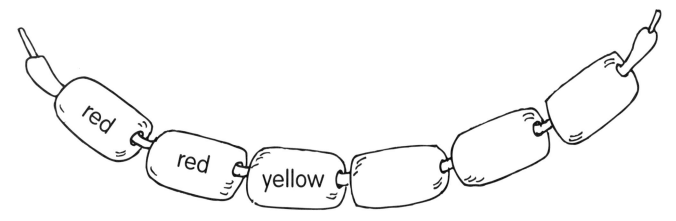

Skills: Read color words; make a pattern.

Read and Understand with Leveled Texts, Grade K • EMC 3440 • © Evan-Moor Corp.

Words That Rhyme

Circle the words that rhyme in each row.

  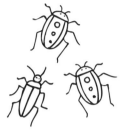

| beads | seeds | bed | bugs |

   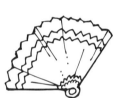

| can | man | cat | fan |

| bed | thread | bread | bear |

| one | bird | glue | shoe |

Skill: Identify rhyming words. **101**

Picture Dictionary

head

hand

mitt

ball

The Ballgame

Name

1

One head, one hat,

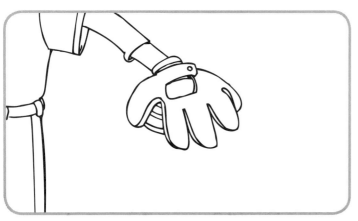

One hand, one mitt,

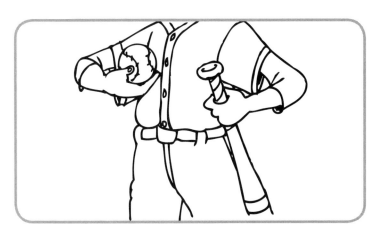

One ball, one bat,

One swing, one hit,

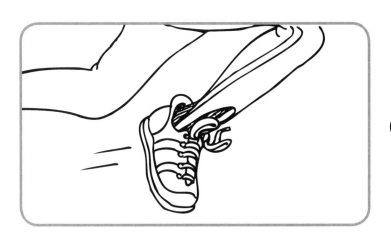

One foot, one shoe,

One run for you!

Name _____

Remembering the Story

Cut and glue the pictures in order. Tell the story.

1

glue

2

glue

3

glue

4

glue

One ball,
one bat,

One swing,
one hit,

One run
for you!

One head,
one hat,

Read and Understand with Leveled Texts, Grade K • EMC 3440 • © Evan-Moor Corp.

Same Sound .... Mm

Color the pictures that begin like **mitt**.

Read and Understand with Leveled Texts, Grade K • EMC 3440 • © Evan-Moor Corp.

Skill: Letter/sound association. **105**

What Do You Need?

Cut and glue to show the things you need.

Things for a Ballgame

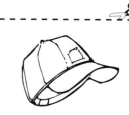

Things for Swimming

Skills: Classify; practice critical thinking.

Read and Understand with Leveled Texts, Grade K • EMC 3440 • © Evan-Moor Corp.

Make a Mini-Book

Draw, color, cut, and staple to make your own little book.

The Ballgame

_____
Name

a ball

a bat

a mitt

a hat

Come play a game.

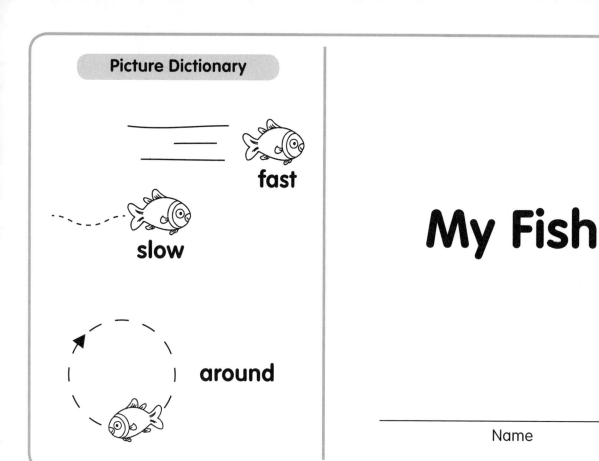

fast

slow

around

My Fish

_____
Name

1

fast

slow

My fish swim and play.
Fast and slow they go.

My fish swim and play.
In and out they go.

My fish swim and play.
All around they go.

Remembering the Story

Color and cut out the fish.
Tape each fish to a straw.
Use the fish puppets to tell the story.

Skill: Retell a story.

Name _____

Find the Opposites

Read each sentence. Color, cut, and glue to show the opposites.

glue	glue
It is fast.	It is slow.

glue	glue
It is in.	It is out.

Skill: Identify opposites. **111**

Color Fun

Read the words. Color the fish.

Skill: Read color words.

Read and Understand with Leveled Texts, Grade K • EMC 3440 • © Evan-Moor Corp.

Big or Little?

Cut and glue to answer the questions.

What is big?	What is little?
glue	glue
glue	glue
glue	glue

Skills: Classify; practice critical thinking.   **113**

Picture Dictionary

 daddy

 mommy

 baby

 sister

 brother

In the Car

_____
Name

Daddy sings.
Mommy drives.

Baby cries.
Sister colors.

Brother reads.
And I sleep.

Remembering the Story

Cut and glue to tell what they did.

 Daddy
glue

 Mommy
glue

 Baby
glue

 Sister
glue

 Brother
glue

drives
cries
colors
sings
reads

Read and Understand with Leveled Texts, Grade K • EMC 3440 • © Evan-Moor Corp.

Name _____

Noisy or Quiet?

Is it noisy or quiet?
Draw a line to match.

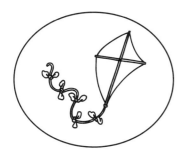

noisy

quiet

Read and Understand with Leveled Texts, Grade K • EMC 3440 • © Evan-Moor Corp.

Skills: Identify opposites; practice word meaning; practice critical thinking.   **117**

The -*ing* Family

Write the words. Cut and glue to show what each word means.

| s + ing | --------------------------------- | glue |

| w + ing | --------------------------------- | glue |

| r + ing | --------------------------------- | glue |

| k + ing | --------------------------------- | glue |

Name _____

When Would You Do It?

Cut and glue.

night   day

glue	glue
glue	glue
glue	glue

 sleep

 read

 look

 run

 jump

 ride

 hats

_____ line

drum

Get in Line

_____
Name

1

We have hats.
We can ride.
We will get in line.

I have a drum.
I can play.
I will get in line.

We are ready.
Come with us.
You can get in line.

Name _____

Remembering the Story

Match each picture with a word.

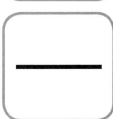

• hats

• line

• drum

Draw a line of funny hats.

Skills: Recall story details; practice word meaning.

Read and Understand with Leveled Texts, Grade K • EMC 3440 • © Evan-Moor Corp.

The -at Family

Write the words.

c + at	- -
b + at	- -
m + at	- -
r + at	- -
f + at	- -

Draw a **cat** and a **bat**.

Draw a **fat rat** on a **mat**.

Name _____

Match the Shapes

Cut and glue to match the shapes.

glue

glue

glue

glue

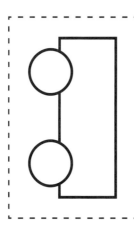
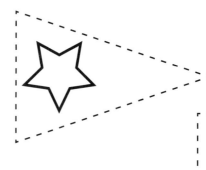

I like you!

Read and Understand with Leveled Texts, Grade K • EMC 3440 • © Evan-Moor Corp.

Same Words

Circle the words in each row that are the same as the first word in the row.

come	come	come	cat	come
go	mom	go	go	mat
line	line	will	line	line
am	ant	am	and	am
have	have	the	hat	have

Cut and glue to make a sentence.

| glue | glue | glue |

| with | us. | Come |

● one

● ● two

● ● ● three

● ● ● ● four

● ● ● ● ● five

● ● ● ● ● ● six

Count the Pups

_____
Name

One pup in the yard.　　**Two** pups in the car.

Three pups in the house. **Four** pups in the barn.

Five pups in a pen. **Six** pups in a pile.

Remembering the Story

Cut and glue to tell how many.

pups in the car . . . .

glue

pups in the barn . . . .

glue

pups in a pen . . . .

glue

pups in the yard . . . .

glue

pups in the house . . . .

glue

pups in a pile . . . .

glue

1	**2**	**3**	**4**	**5**	**6**
one	two	three	four	five	six

Skills: Recall story details; read number words; match number words to numerals.

Read and Understand with Leveled Texts, Grade K • EMC 3440 • © Evan-Moor Corp.

Name _____

Same Sound .... Pp

Color the pictures that begin like **pup**.

How many did you find?

Skill: Letter/sound association.   **129**

S at the End

Circle the correct word to fill in the blank.

I see one _____.

      pup   pups

I see three _____.

      car   cars

I see two _____.

      house   houses

I see six _____.

      bug   bugs

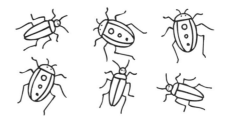

I see one _____.

      cat   cats

Where Are They?

Write to tell where the animals are.

| in the pond | in the grass |
| on the dock | in the tree |

Where is the bird? _____

Where are the ducks? _____

Where are the cats? _____

Where is the boy? _____

Read and Understand with Leveled Texts, Grade K • EMC 3440 • © Evan-Moor Corp.

Skills: Answer questions to match text to pictures. **131**

Picture Dictionary

 duck   truck

 kitten   mitten

 man   can

What Do You See?

_____
Name

1

I see a duck with a truck.
What do you see?

I see a kitten with a mitten.
What do you see?

I see a man with a can.
What do you see?

Remembering the Story

Color, cut, and glue to match rhyming words from the story.

duck

glue

kitten

glue

man

glue

Skills: Recall story details; identify rhyming words.

Read and Understand with Leveled Texts, Grade K • EMC 3440 • © Evan-Moor Corp.

The *-an* Family

Write the words.

m + an = ____ ____ ____   r + an = ____ ____ ____

c + an = ____ ____ ____   t + an = ____ ____ ____

f + an = ____ ____ ____   v + an = ____ ____ ____

Use the words
to fill in the blanks.

The _____ has a _____.

The dog _____.

The _____ is in a _____.

It has a _____.

Skills: Word family activity; practice word meaning.

Rhyming Pairs

Color, cut, and glue to show pairs that rhyme.

| glue |

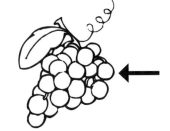 ←

| glue |

| glue |

| glue |

| glue |

 ←

| glue |

Read and Understand with Leveled Texts, Grade K • EMC 3440 • © Evan-Moor Corp.

Name _____

Real or Make-Believe?

Could it be real? Circle **yes** or **no**.

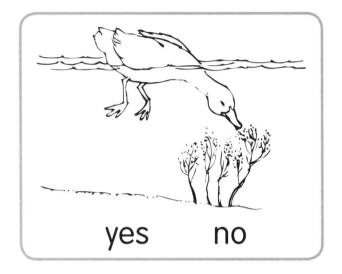

yes   no

yes   no

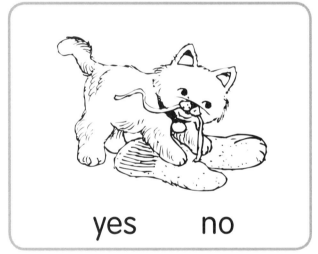

yes   no

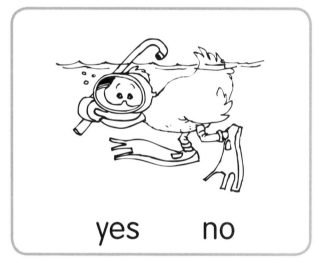

yes   no

yes   no

yes   no

Read and Understand with Leveled Texts, Grade K • EMC 3440 • © Evan-Moor Corp.

Skill: Distinguish between real and make-believe.   **137**

read

quack

home

Little Quackers

_____
Name

I can read here.
It is quiet.

Please do not quack.

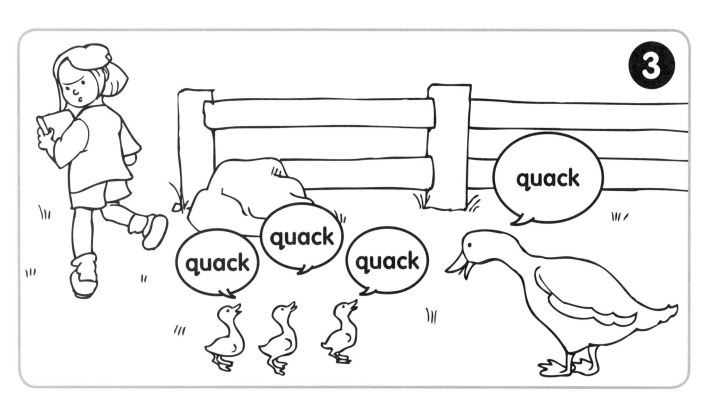

I cannot read here.
I will go home.

Name _____

Remembering the Story

Cut and glue to tell what each character said.

glue

glue

glue

Please do
not quack.

quack
quack
quack

quack

Skill: Recall story details.

Read and Understand with Leveled Texts, Grade K • EMC 3440 • © Evan-Moor Corp.

Same Sound ····················· **qu**

Cut and glue the pictures that begin like **quack**.

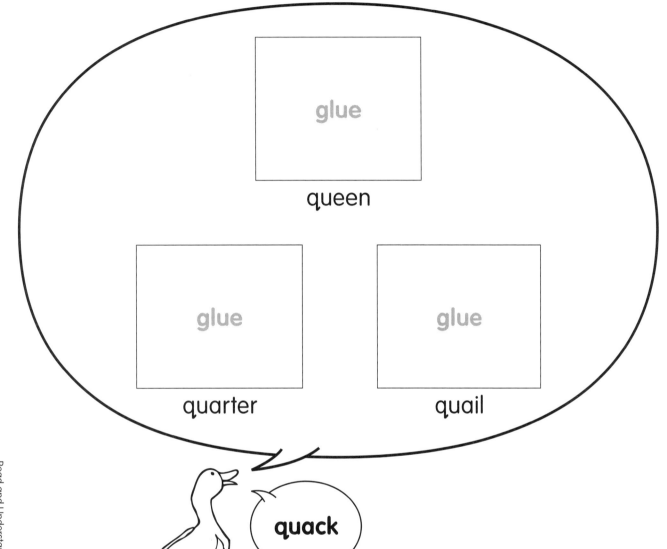

Skill: Letter/sound association.

Make a Duck

Color, cut, fold, and glue to make a duck.

body

yellow

fold

glue

bill

fold

orange

head

glue

yellow

Name _____

Noisy Ones

Draw to show what or who might make each sound.

moo

quack

woof-woof

meow

grrrrrr

quiet

Skill: Practice critical thinking.   **143**

Picture Dictionary

sunny

fly

kite

My Kite

_____
Name

1

It is sunny.
I can fly my kite.

Look! I can fly my kite.
My kite is up.

It is not sunny now.
My kite is down.

My Kite

Remembering the Story

Cut and glue to put the pictures in order.
Tell the story.

1

2

3

| glue | glue | glue |

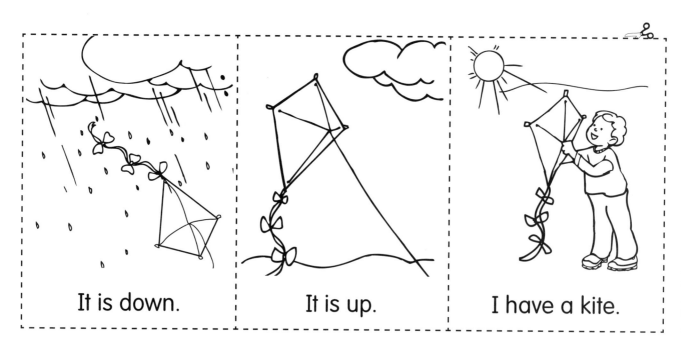

It is down.

It is up.

I have a kite.

Read and Understand with Leveled Texts, Grade K • EMC 3440 • © Evan-Moor Corp.

Name _____

Same Sound ·················· **Rr**

Cut and glue the pictures that begin like **rain**.

Skill: Letter/sound association.   **147**

What Can You Do?

Draw and tell what you can do each day.

Sunny Day

Look! I can _____.

Rainy Day

Look! I can _____.

Skills: Practice critical thinking; prewriting activity.

Read and Understand with Leveled Texts, Grade K • EMC 3440 • © Evan-Moor Corp.

What's in the Sky?

Connect the dots to see what's in the sky.
Start at **1**.

Skills: Practice small motor skills; follow directions.

 **go up**

 **come down**

 **slip and slide**

We Have Fun

_____
Name

1

We stop and go.
We go and stop.
Here we are up on the top.

We go up.
We come down.
We slip and slide all around.

Come play with us.
We have fun.
We like to play in the sun.

Name _____

Remembering the Story

Cut and glue to put the pictures in order.
Tell the story.

| glue | glue | glue |

We have fun in the sun.

I slip and slide.

I come down.

I go up.

Read and Understand with Leveled Texts, Grade K • EMC 3440 • © Evan-Moor Corp.

Same Sound..................... **Tt**

Cut and glue the pictures that begin like **top**.

glue	glue	glue

glue

glue

glue

glue

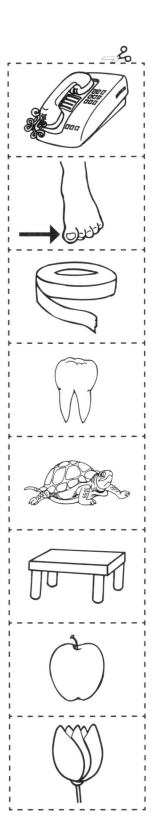

Which Is It?

Cut and glue to show **stop** and **go**.

stop

glue	glue	glue

go

glue	glue	glue

Skills: Practice word meaning; identify opposites.

Read and Understand with Leveled Texts, Grade K • EMC 3440 • © Evan-Moor Corp.

Name _____

Fun in the Sun

Draw four ways you have fun in the sun.
Tell about the pictures.

Read and Understand with Leveled Texts, Grade K • EMC 3440 • © Evan-Moor Corp.

Skill: Prewriting activity. **155**

Answer Key

Page 8

Page 9

one   two
two   one
one   two

Page 10

5 items begin with **Ss**:
sun, seven, seal, saddle, six

Page 11

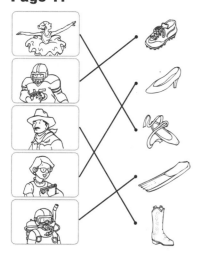

Page 14

We go up. (Glue children climbing up steps of slide here.)

We go down. (Glue children sliding down the slide here.)

Page 15

up   down
up   up

Page 16

Shapes are colored as labeled and matched correctly.

Page 17

Drawings must show meanings of **up** and **down**.

Page 20

I get my coat.
I get my hat.
I get my dad.

Page 21

See my coat.
(Glue coat here.)

See my hat.
(Glue hat here.)

Page 22

Students trace to show the path down the hill.

Page 23

5 items begin with **Dd**:
dinosaur, dog, doll, door, duck

Page 26

cat, dog, lizard
dog, cat
lizard

Answers will vary.

Page 27

dog: doghouse
fish: fishbowl
hamster: tank

Page 28

car, caterpillar, comb, corn, carrot, can

Page 29

Cat and rug are colored as labeled.

Page 32

play with a toy mouse
toy mouse
sleeps

Page 33

juggler, jet, jar, jacks, juice box

Page 34

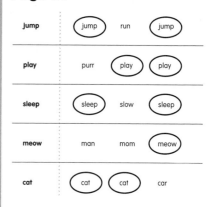

Page 35

Drawings and answers will vary.

Page 38

bed
nest
den

Drawings will vary.

Page 39

5 items begin with **Bb**:
bear, button, bed, balloon, book

Page 40

Page 41

❶ a blue balloon
❷ a yellow triangle
❸ a happy face
❹ a red bed

Answers will vary.

Page 44

wagon, plane, car

rode in wagon: doll, bear
rode in plane: girl, bear, doll
rode in car: dad, girl

Page 45
worm, wolf, walrus

Page 46
Objects are colored as directed.

Page 47
wagon, plane, bike, horse, car, skateboard

Page 50
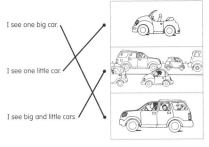

Drawings will vary.

Page 51
4 hats	2 wagons
1 wagon	1 car
3 cars	1 hat

Page 52
The words **big** and **little** are traced.

big elephant (colored gray)
little bugs (colored red)

Page 53
leaf, lamp, llama, lock, lunchbox, log

Page 56

Page 57
Drawings and sentences will vary.

Page 58
hop, shop
stop, mop
top, pop

Page 59
a stop sign (colored red)

Page 62

Drawings will vary.

Page 63
cat, bat, rat, mat

Page 64
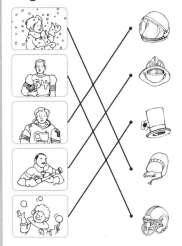

Page 65
6 items begin with **Hh**:
hand, house, helicopter, hippo, hammer, hamburger

Page 68
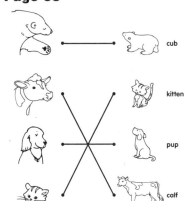

Page 69
no	no
yes	yes
no	yes

Page 70
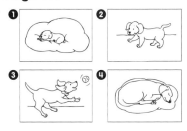

Page 71
Pictures and results will vary.

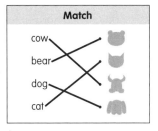

Page 74
❶ tie shoe
❷ use glue
❸ read

Drawings will vary.

Page 75
Drawings and sentences will vary.

Page 76

❶   **❷**

❸   **❹**

Page 77
glue, moo
boohoo, shoe
screw, ah choo
coo, goo goo

Page 80
truck
help us

Drawings will vary.

Page 81
5 items begin with **tr**: trunk,
trumpet, trophy, train, tree

Page 82

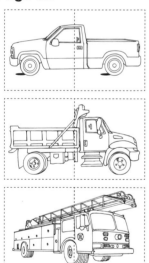

Page 83
Find **truck** 5 times.

firetruck
pickup truck
dump truck

Page 86
yes, yes, no

Drawing shows a picture of
Mom getting wet.

Page 87
car   jar
star   bar

Drawings will vary.

Page 88

Page 89
Drawings and stories
will vary.

Page 92
Fruit is colored as labeled.

Page 93
yarn, yogurt, yo-yo, yolk,
yak, yawn

Page 94

red	run	red	red
yellow	yellow	yarn	yellow
blue	ball	blue	blue
orange	orange	orange	jump
green	get	green	green
purple	purple	play	purple

Page 95
five   two
four   one
three   six

Objects are colored as
labeled.

Page 98
Beads create the pattern:
red, blue, red, blue, red, blue,
red, blue

Page 99
            two
three   one
two   six
five   four

Beads are colored as labeled.

Page 100
Beads are colored to make
the patterns:

red, green; red, green;
red, green

blue, yellow; blue, yellow;
blue, yellow

red, red, yellow; red, red, yellow

Page 101
beads, seeds
can, man, fan
bed, thread, bread
glue, shoe

Page 104

① One head, one hat,

② One ball, one bat,

③ One swing, one hit,

④ One run for you!

Page 105
5 items begin with **Mm**:
monkey, mailbox, mitten, milk, map

Page 106
Things for a Ballgame:
cap, ball, shoe, mitt

Things for Swimming:
swimsuits, inner tube, goggles

Page 107
Drawings and results will vary.

Page 110
Students retell the story using the puppets they made.

Page 111
fast: speedboat
slow: rowboat
in: turtle in shell
out: turtle out of shell

Page 112
Fish are colored as labeled.

Page 113
What is big?
dinosaur, elephant, whale

What is little?
bees, mice, birds

Page 116
daddy **sings**
mommy **drives**
baby **cries**
sister **colors**
brother **reads**

Page 117
noisy: horn player, radio, crying baby, firetruck

quiet: painter, butterfly, turtle, kite

Page 118
sing
wing
ring
king

Pictures and words match.

Page 119
night: sleep, read, look
day: run, jump, ride

Page 122
drum
hats
line

Drawings will vary.

Page 123
cat
bat
mat
rat
fat

Drawings may vary but must match instructions.

Page 124

I like you!

Page 125

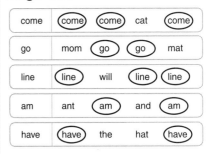

come	(come)	(come)	cat	(come)
go	mom	(go)	(go)	mat
line	(line)	will	(line)	(line)
am	ant	(am)	and	(am)
have	(have)	the	hat	(have)

Come with us.

Page 128
2, 4, 5, 1, 3, 6

Page 129
6 items begin with **Pp**:
popcorn, pocket, pumpkin, pizza, pencil, paint

Page 130
pup, cars, houses, bugs, cat

Page 131
in the tree
in the pond
in the grass
on the dock

Page 134
truck
mitten
can

Page 135
man   ran
can   tan
fan   van

The **man** has a **can**.
The dog **ran**.

The **man** is in a **van**.
It has a **fan**.

Page 136

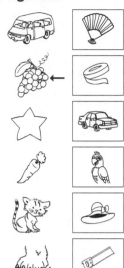

Page 137

yes   no
yes   no
no   no

Page 140

Page 141

Pictures and words match.

Page 142

Duck is made as directed.

Page 143

cow	duck
dog	cat
Answers	a person
may vary.	

Page 146

❶ I have a kite.
❷ It is up.
❸ It is down.

Page 147

rabbit, ring, rake, rocket, rock,
robot, rooster

Page 148

Drawings and sentences
will vary.

Page 149

a kite

Page 152

❶ I go up.
❷ I come down.
❸ I slip and slide.

Page 153

telephone, toe, tape, tooth,
turtle, table, tulip

Page 154

Page 155

Drawings will vary.